In loving memory of Jim Haskins—K.B.

Acknowledgment
Many thanks to U.S. Congressman John Lewis and his office for their assistance and advice.

Bibliography
Lewis, John, with Michael D'Orso. *Walking with the Wind: A Memoir of the Movement.*
    New York: Simon & Schuster, 1998.
———. "The Living Legacy and Influence of Dr. Martin Luther King, Jr." Sermon at Urban
    Ministry Conference, First Presbyterian Church of Atlanta, Georgia, January 18, 2003.
———. Transcript of interview with Jim Haskins, May 6, 2004.

Manufactured in China

Book design by Design Press

Design Press is a division
of the Savannah College
of Art and Design

Book production by The Kids at Our House

The text is set in Frutiger
The illustrations are rendered in oils and fabric collage

10 9 8 7 6 5 4 3 2 1
First Edition

Library of Congress Cataloging-in-Publication Data
Haskins, James.
John Lewis in the lead: a story of the civil rights movement / Jim Haskins and Kathleen Benson ;
illustrations by Benny Andrews.— 1st ed.
p. cm.
Summary: "A biography of John Lewis, Georgia Congressman and one of the 'Big Six' civil rights
leaders of the 1960s, focusing on his youth and culminating in the voter registration drives that
sparked 'Bloody Sunday,' as hundreds of people walked across the Edmund Pettus Bridge in Selma,
Alabama. Includes timeline of Lewis's life"—Provided by publisher.
    ISBN-13: 978-1-58430-250-6   ISBN-10: 1-58430-250-X
1. Lewis, John, 1940 Feb. 21—Juvenile literature. 2. Legislators—United States—Biography—Juvenile
literature. 3. African American legislators—Biography—Juvenile literature. 4. United States. Congress.
House—Biography—Juvenile literature. 5. Civil rights workers—United States—Biography—Juvenile
literature. 6. African American civil rights workers—Biography—Juvenile literature. 7. Student Nonviolent
Coordinating Committee (U.S.)—Biography—Juvenile literature. 8. African Americans—Civil rights—
Juvenile literature. 9. Civil rights movements—Southern States—History—20th century—Juvenile
literature. I. Benson, Kathleen. II. Andrews, Benny, ill. III. Title.
E840.8.L43H37 2006
323.092—dc22   2005035472

JOHN LEWIS IN THE LEAD

A Story of the Civil Rights Movement

Jim Haskins and **Kathleen Benson**

illustrations by **Benny Andrews**

Lee & Low Books Inc.

New York

JOHN LEWIS

was born at a time when the winds of change were blowing, just waiting for someone to catch them and hold on long enough for everyone to feel the breeze.

It was another wind altogether that blew one day when John was a little boy. He was playing in the dirt yard of his Aunt Seneva's house with many of his brothers, sisters, and cousins. The sky began to cloud over and the wind started to pick up. In the distance lightning flashed. Then came a loud clap of thunder and a torrent of rain.

"Come inside quick, children," said Aunt Seneva, and she hustled them all into her small wooden house.

Inside Aunt Seneva and the children huddled together, hushed, listening to the wind howl and feeling the house shake. Suddenly they felt the floor move. The wind was so strong it lifted the corner of the house, trying to pull them into the sky.

Aunt Seneva started to cry, and the children began to sob too. Then Aunt Seneva gathered her courage. "Everybody hold hands!" she called, and the frightened children did as they were told. "Now, we got to walk over to that corner." They hurried to the corner, and the combined weight of their bodies settled the house back down.

Soon another corner began to lift from the force of the wind, so they rushed to that corner. Each time the wind lifted part of the house, Aunt Seneva and the children held it down with the weight of their bodies. Holding hands, they walked with the wind until the danger had passed.

The storm didn't last long, but John never forgot that day.

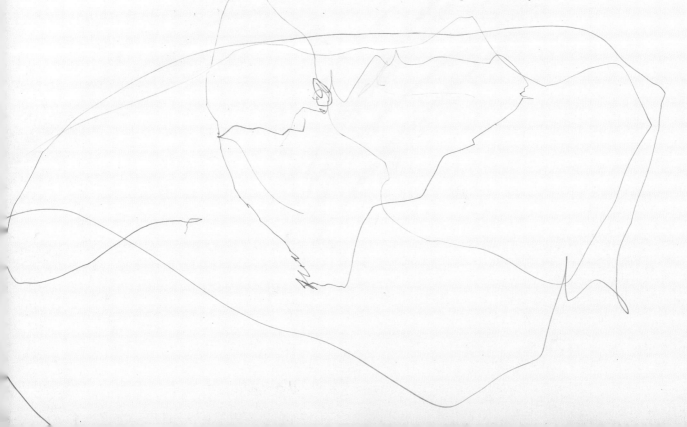

In 1945, when John turned five, he was put in charge of his family's chickens. He had to take care of about sixty animals on the farm near Troy, Alabama, where his family lived as sharecroppers. They worked on a white man's land in return for a place to live and a share of the crops they grew.

John was happy and proud to have this job. He liked chickens and took his responsibility very seriously. He carried buckets of feed to the henhouse. He kept it clean. He named each chicken. Two of his favorites were Big Belle and L'il Pullet.

At night, to quiet the chickens, John preached to them. He wanted to be a minister, and this was a good way to practice. John's habit of giving sermons in the chicken coop earned him the nickname Preacher.

During the time John was growing up, the South was segregated. Black people were kept apart from white people. It was against the law for blacks to eat in white restaurants. Black children could not go to the same schools as white children. Black people had to sit in the backs of public buses and give up their seats to whites if the "white seats" in the front were filled.

John realized that segregation was keeping his family from having a better life. This made him angry, but his parents warned John to stay quiet. "Don't get in trouble," they said. "Don't get in the way."

One day when he was fifteen, John heard Dr. Martin Luther King, Jr. on the radio. Dr. King was a preacher in Montgomery, Alabama, and he was talking about the bus boycott. Black people in Montgomery had stopped riding the buses to protest bus segregation. When Dr. King said segregation was wrong, John felt as though Dr. King were speaking directly to him, telling him it was time to get in the way. It was time to turn things upside down in order to set them right side up.

Inspired by Dr. King, John took his first steps to protest segregation. He asked for a library card at his county public library, knowing that black people were not allowed to have cards. John was not surprised that the librarian said the library was for whites only. Then he went home and wrote the library a letter of protest.

After graduating from high school in 1957, John went to Nashville, Tennessee, to study to become a minister. He wrote to Dr. King, who invited John to visit Montgomery. When they met, Dr. King said they could fight the injustice of segregation peacefully. He told John to study the life of Mohandas K. Gandhi, who had led nonviolent protests in India.

John liked Gandhi's idea of nonviolent resistance as a way to bring about social change. With this in mind, John organized sit-ins at lunch counters where blacks were not allowed to eat with whites. In 1961 he joined the Student Nonviolent Coordinating Committee (SNCC). The students went on Freedom Rides to challenge segregation at interstate bus terminals. Blacks and whites sat next to each other on buses that traveled from state to state.

John's commitment to nonviolence would soon be tested. In May 1961, a bus carrying John and other Freedom Riders arrived at the Montgomery, Alabama, bus station. John was the first one off the bus. Aside from a group of newspaper reporters, the streets were strangely deserted. John had just begun to deliver a statement to the reporters when suddenly hundreds of white people came running from behind buildings and around corners. Waving baseball bats, boards, bricks, tire irons, hoes, and rakes, they screamed out insults.

"Let's all stand together," John cried, as the mob attacked the Freedom Riders. Someone hit John on the head with a wooden crate, and he fell to the ground. After being treated at a local hospital, John was anxious to rejoin his group and carry on.

The brutal attack was big news, and Dr. King was concerned. He rushed to Montgomery and tried to convince John to protect himself and stop the rides, but John would not. So with a bandaged and bruised John Lewis at his side, Dr. King held a press conference to announce that the Freedom Rides would continue.

Over the next two years, John led many protests. He was often beaten and arrested, but he did not give up. He believed segregation was unjust. He was committed to bringing people together to fight for their civil rights.

In August 1963 John was invited to speak at the March on Washington for Jobs and Freedom. The gathering was intended to make Congress pass a civil rights bill that would guarantee equal rights for black people.

Twenty-three-year-old John Lewis was the youngest speaker on the steps of the Lincoln Memorial that day. He spoke out against segregation

and promised to continue leading nonviolent protests. Dr. King was there too. He delivered his famous "I Have a Dream" speech, expressing the hope that one day all Americans would be free to enjoy equal rights and opportunities.

new slide

The March on Washington had an impact. The following year President Lyndon B. Johnson signed the Civil Rights Act of 1964, making racial discrimination in restaurants, bus stations, and other public places illegal and requiring equal employment opportunities for all citizens.

John now turned his attention to voters' rights. With his help, SNCC made plans to register southern black people to vote. It would be a hard task. Many white people could not bear the thought of black people having the freedom to vote. They felt threatened, and feared that blacks would gain political power over them.

In January 1965 John went to Selma, Alabama. More than fifteen thousand black adults were eligible to vote in the county where Selma was located, but only about three hundred were registered. John and other SNCC workers began leading groups of people to the city courthouse in Selma to register to vote. Each time a group arrived, the clerk hung up a sign that read: OUT TO LUNCH. It didn't matter what time of day they arrived. The sign always went up.

The groups waited outside the courthouse without complaint, hour after hour, all day long. People grew tired. Their feet hurt. But they remained dignified and calm. John encouraged them, praising their courage to endure the boredom as well as the threat of violence.

Jim Clark, the sheriff of Selma, was determined not to let blacks register to vote. When he realized they would continue to wait to enter the courthouse, Sheriff Clark ordered his officers to block the entrance. During three days of peaceful protests, more than two hundred people were arrested, including John.

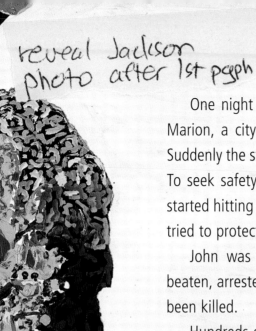

One night after a rally to support people trying to register to vote in Marion, a city near Selma, a group started marching to the courthouse. Suddenly the streetlights went out and police began attacking the marchers. To seek safety, a woman and her son ran into a small cafe. A policeman started hitting the woman, and her son, Jimmie Lee Jackson, was shot as he tried to protect her. He died soon after.

John was heartbroken when he heard the news. People had been beaten, arrested, and jailed during their protests, but until now no one had been killed.

Hundreds of people crowded into the church to hear Dr. King preach at Jimmie Lee Jackson's funeral. Afterward, John walked with Dr. King and a thousand other mourners to the graveyard. Along the way someone suggested that they keep walking right to Montgomery, the state capital, and deposit the casket on the capitol steps. Jimmie was buried in Marion that day, but back in Selma many people liked the idea of a march to Montgomery.

Montgomery was fifty-four miles from Selma. Fear mixed with excitement at the idea of a march that would take about five days. There were also rumors that Alabama governor George Wallace would let state troopers do whatever was necessary to prevent the Selma-to-Montgomery march. Dr. King was supposed to lead the marchers, but after receiving threats on his life, he asked his close ally, Reverend Hosea Williams, to take his place.

Late in the afternoon on Sunday, March 7, 1965, John Lewis and Reverend Williams stood at the head of a group of nearly six hundred people. From Brown Chapel AME Church they marched down Sylvan Street, turned right on Water Street, then walked to Broad Street. There they turned left and headed up the steep western arch of the Edmund Pettus Bridge, which led out of Selma. Several dozen of Sheriff Clark's men watched the marchers as they passed.

At the crest of the bridge, John suddenly saw a sea of state troopers spread out across the highway. On either side and behind them were more of Sheriff Clark's men, some riding horses.

The commander of the troopers, Major John Cloud, raised his bullhorn. "This is an unlawful assembly," he boomed. "You are ordered to disperse and go back to your church or your homes."

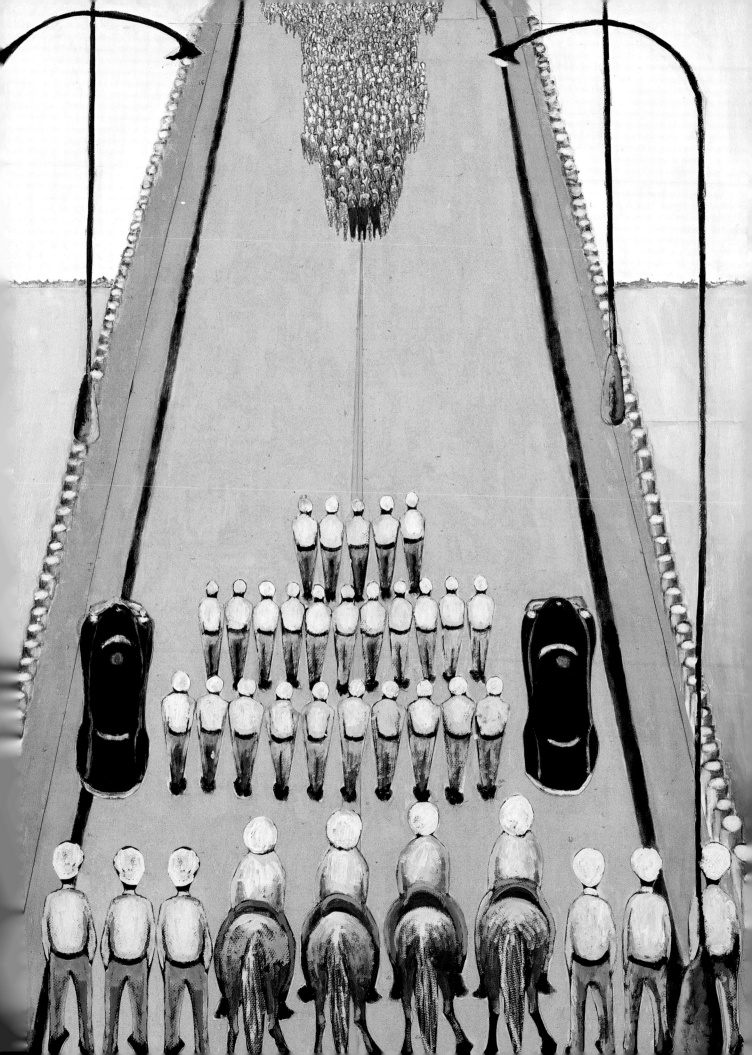

John stood at the top of the bridge. Ahead of him was the swarm of state troopers. Below him swirled the brown water of the river. All around were crowds of screaming, jeering people, their faces contorted with hate. And behind him were hundreds of courageous but frightened marchers—mothers and fathers, teenagers and teachers, beauticians and undertakers, farmers and mechanics.

Again Major Cloud raised the bullhorn to his lips. "You have two minutes to turn around and go back to your church," he shouted.

John believed that everyone should have the right to vote and that they should not back down. But he saw they were trapped. They could not turn around—there were too many people on the bridge. They could not go forward either. That was inviting an attack by the state troopers. John could feel the marchers begin to panic. He knew they were waiting for him to tell them what to do.

Standing at the crest of the Edmund Pettus Bridge, John remembered the way his Aunt Seneva had taught him to walk with the wind. He remembered that people can survive any storm if they stick together.

"We should all pray," John told Reverend Williams. The reverend was thinking much the same thing. He asked Major Cloud if they could have a moment to pray.

Just as those at the front of the march bowed their heads, and just one minute after his two-minute warning, Major Cloud gave the order to attack. A wave of state troopers charged up the bridge.

His head bowed in prayer, John heard the sounds of terror—the pounding of horses' hooves and troopers' heavy boots, the shouts and screams of men and women, the cries of frightened people trying to pray and be brave.

Suddenly a trooper swung his club at John, knocking him to the ground. John tried to protect his head as the trooper hit him again.

Other marchers at the front of the group took blows too. Those behind them turned to go back, but there were so many people on the bridge it was hard to move.

As the marchers tried to get away from the troopers, they were attacked by more of Sheriff Clark's men. The mob also attacked cameramen and reporters, but they couldn't stop them from reporting the violence. The pictures and television broadcasts of state troopers and policemen beating defenseless people brought the country face-to-face with the riot that would soon be known as Bloody Sunday.

Although John was badly injured, he somehow made it back to Brown Chapel that night. The church and surrounding area were filled with people protesting what had happened on the bridge. John managed to speak to the crowd, and he asked President Johnson to protect the marchers whose only desire was to register to vote. Then John allowed himself to be taken to the hospital.

John had a serious head injury, a concussion. In the hospital, his feelings of helplessness were as bad as the physical pain. He didn't know what was going on outside. He wanted to know what had happened to the people on the bridge.

Finally reports began to trickle in. Bloody Sunday was a national scandal. There were demonstrations in more than eighty cities against the brutality of the Alabama police and troopers. There were calls for a federal law that would guarantee everyone the right to vote. By the time John was released from the hospital, he had real hope that black people would soon have the same voting rights as whites.

John joined with Dr. King and other civil rights leaders to show Alabama and the nation that they would not give up. A new date, Sunday, March 21, was set for a march from Selma to Montgomery. Word soon came that religious leaders, elected officials, celebrities, and ordinary people from across the country planned to join the march in support of voting rights for all Americans.

This time, under the protection of federal troops, more than three thousand people started out from Selma. Over five days the sun burned down on the marchers and rain fell in torrents, but no one complained, no one gave up. "We felt bonded with one another, with the people we passed, with the entire nation," John recalled. By the time the marchers reached Montgomery, they were twenty-five thousand strong.

Five months later President Johnson signed the Voting Rights Act of 1965, which protected the rights of all Americans to vote. The act made it a crime to use force against anyone trying to register and vote.

In 1986, twenty-one years after that historic act was passed, the votes of both black and white citizens elected John Lewis to the United States House of Representatives, where he continues to serve today as a congressman from Georgia.

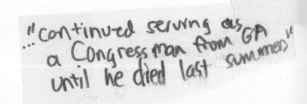

The Life and Times of John Lewis

1940   February 21: Born near Troy, Alabama

1955   December 5–December 21, 1956: Bus boycott in Montgomery, Alabama, which led to U.S. Supreme Court decision declaring segregation on public transportation illegal

1956   Denied library card from Pike County (Alabama) Public Library

1957   Graduated from Pike County Training School, Brundidge, Alabama

1961   Joined Student Nonviolent Coordinating Committee (SNCC)
Participated in Freedom Rides that challenged segregation at interstate bus terminals
Graduated from American Baptist Theological Seminary, Nashville, Tennessee

1963   Elected chairman of SNCC
Graduated from Fisk University, Nashville, Tennessee, with BA degree in religion and philosophy
August 28: Spoke at Lincoln Memorial during March on Washington for Jobs and Freedom; estimated 250,000 people attended

Frances Miller / Time and Life Pictures / Getty Images

John Lewis (front, second from left) links arms with protestors to lead a march in Cambridge, Maryland, May, 1964

1964   Coordinated SNCC voter registration drives during Mississippi Freedom Summer project
July 2: Civil Rights Act, which prohibited discrimination in public facilities, government, and employment, signed into law

1965   March 7: With Reverend Hosea Williams, led first Selma-to-Montgomery March across the Edmund Pettus Bridge, which culminated in Bloody Sunday
March 21–March 25: With other civil rights leaders, led third Selma-to-Montgomery March for voting rights; 25,000 people participated
August 6: Voting Rights Act, which provided for federal registration of voters and guaranteed every citizen the right to vote, signed into law

1966   Resigned as chairman of SNCC
Continued civil rights work as associate director of the Field Foundation

1967   Appointed director of Southern Regional Council's Community Organization Project

Courtesy of the Library of Congress

John Lewis speaks to the American Society of Newspaper Editors, 1964

John Lewis (front, right) joins in prayer with Dr. Martin Luther King, Jr. and other civil rights leaders at the third Selma-to-Montgomery March, 1965

1968 December: Married Lillian Miles

1970 Appointed executive director of Southern Regional Council's Voter Education Project (VEP)

1976 May: Son John Miles Lewis born

1977 Appointed to head ACTION, the federal volunteer agency, by President Jimmy Carter

1981 Elected to city council of Atlanta, Georgia

1986 November 4: Elected to U.S. House of Representatives as Democrat from Georgia's Fifth Congressional District; reelected every four years since then

1990 Named one of eleven "rising stars in Congress" by *National Journal*

1996 Selma-to-Montgomery National Historic Trail designated by President Bill Clinton

1998 *Walking with the Wind: A Memoir of the Movement*, Lewis's story of the civil rights movement, published
        Presented with library card by Pike County Public Library

2001 Received John F. Kennedy Profile in Courage Award for Lifetime Achievement, in recognition of his career marked by courage, leadership, vision, and commitment to human rights

Congressman Lewis at his home in Atlanta, Georgia, late 1980s

Congressman Lewis in front of the United States Capitol, Washington, DC, 2005